61 Central

poems of

Ink

Finishing Line Press
Georgetown, Kentucky

61 Central

with apologies and gratitude

Publisher: Leah Maines
Editor: Christen Kincaid
Cover Art: Andrew Feindt
Author Photo: John Posada
Cover Design: Elizabeth Maines McCleavy

Printed in the USA on acid-free paper.
Order online: www.finishinglinepress.com
              also available on amazon.com

Author inquiries and mail orders:
Finishing Line Press
P. O. Box 1626
Georgetown, Kentucky 40324
U. S. A.

Table of Contents

avoiding eye contact

Avoiding eye contact—
shy for clouded nest
in twisted hills—
is the town.

Before the town,
winds the road—
flat, waving limb
double-ended in open,
invisibly upright palm.

On the road,
markings—
travel dividers, devisors—
assure order,
while wayside signs
rust in peace.

Since turning onto this stretch,
the town's private driveway,
no headlights have come
—wide-eyed, beaming—
to greet me,
none framed in rearview
nor nuzzled my back bumper
to hasten their return home.

Plowmen's Lament

Paid by neighboring town,
plowman grinds metal against asphalt
for seven twisting miles,
keeps 61 North clear
of snow and ice.

Paid by neighboring town,
plowman grinds metal against asphalt
for seven twisting miles,
keeps 61 South clear
of snow and ice.

61 Central—
infernal creation—
clears itself.

Every winter storm,
in parallel,
unknowing unison,
both plowmen keep miles of road—
the approach—
salted, smooth.

The end of their obligation—
flashing orange beacons,
reflective Road Closed signs—
signal cooperation's end—
barriers to respective directions;
an in-between that will never bear tracks
of any but its own tread.

enabled by salt,
this much is obvious:
no-one is home—

streets lead into themselves—
by. way. of. stop. signs;
hinged asphalt

lifeless electronic signals—
the only landmarks
not secretly burning

under white blanket,
walkways stalk the past unaware
their stares no longer discernible

Alongside warped and buckled roads
pitted with potholes,
sporadic gutters betray (what were) sidewalks
burrowing into snow, earth.

Melt runs into invisible sewers;
flow, inspired by 48°February,
babblesngwheream
igoingwhereamIg
oingwherea
migoingw
hereamig
oingw
here?

Lacking surveying equipment,
there's no vocabulary to respond;
sewer system blueprints
read like universals.

Eventually,
you make it a point to stop listening.

Eventually,
it's impossible.

remaining: two feet—
foundation sprouting rusty rebar;
spider-legged branches reach,
bowed low by iced joints and white flake;
failed attempts—
scattered web of skeleton claws
broken trying to yank barb
from concrete skin;
lion stops roaring,
slips into peaceful slumber.

deeper
in inch-thick white
melting
by increasing degrees

my initial stride
off pummeled path—
snow sure

until

brown pocket
burrow
(what would dig down

(...undaunted)

) footprints forward,
between, trees
black with wet

boughs writhe,
recoil from fog
-filtered sun

no means to ask health
(break a limb)— no courage,
no knowledge

is that vowel
consonant
(mongrel string of woe?)

one step between
two steps between— among
them

(dance)

discovering divots
deep scoops
craters cradling dry roots—

(exposed—
out-) stretched

steam speaks
warm whispers—
not warnings but

) evaporated babble

190 pounds makes
3 inch impressions
in melting water

what monster made
pressed the Earth so low
so fast to make it smolder (

Where tire tracks do not tread,
where patches of brown grass
creep through asphalt cranial cap,
keep in mind raging blossom below;
safest to walk for slip and fall and break of bone
than by firmer footing follow
and lay forever in fire's bed.

one history

Only did the ground once
open one of its spontaneous mouths to feed—
expose its glowing red throat
to open air
excited by nutrients.

That blackmail,
sacrifice-lust,
denied by extended hand of passerby,
community,
shamed hunger underground.

Grumbles, to this day,
can be heard;
angrily churning stomach
airs frustration,
vents endless rant
—toxic—expiration—
…

in the snow approaching a snowless spot:
deer tracks

in the snow surrounding that same snowless spot:
more snow

On bald hill,
built of sanctioned wreckage, scrape,
overlooking landscaped vegetation
slowly reclaiming abandoned squares
temporarily laurelled with snow,
runoff pools deepen in pockets.

In each puddle, smoke—
sludge, sluggish—
undulates
in trial,
error.

The source
of
such turbulence
indiscernible through
work boot
insulation.

One assumes the coal—
shimmering
slightly,
swimming,
came into instinct
only to tremble,
run.

before heat and hollow found it,
before feet took their careful steps,
dozer treads crawled this hill,
built and followed improvised road
with blades lowered at their ready,
tumbled collapsed spaces—
living rooms
devoid of namesakes,
condensed with keepsakes—
into valleys
to raise higher
unpredictable mountain—
residents;
unidentifiable piles:
puzzle stratum—
broken drywall,
snapped wood,
crushed brick,
humiliated nails,
defeated mortar

perfectly preserved window frame
separated from its wall
presses glass
against dirt below

there are nail holes
where lip meets ledge

neither cries

just stare(s)

a question of moisture

hovering cloud, which mouth is mother?

heaven's grey, descending ceiling?

wanderer's involuntary expiration?

the 21st gram from every fallen snowflake?

this town's un(der)earthly aura?

With blue domes
sweating beneath crosses painted gold,
church atop opposite hill,
across 61 Central,
framed by bare oak trunk sight,
gets closer
the further I step back
and stare.

Whether by double takes
and faulty recollection
or walking backwards
with anxiety magnet,
I stumble upon two graveyards.

There are three windows
visible on church's face
from my vantage
between two (p)lots.

They stare
                    (back).
They stare.

for Haley & Jess

i loved you enough
to write your name in bright orange
on crumbling asphalt
hidden from traffic

upon my return in winter
sentiments returned
my name written
in red

both proclamations
crossed out by ice tracks
compressed by cowards
tires long gone

acrylic and weather withstanding
i'll see you in spring
and every season
until the paint wears off

in surrounding woods
snow-pressed paw prints
start towards 61 Central

slush pool
between empty house plots
staked
by poorly camouflaged
concrete bones

three feet in
the trail vanishe

several histories

those who've returned,
ventured trespass
in different size shoe,
say there's nothing to see,
keep coming.

61 North and South
converge on central stretch,
abandoned— by death or buy out—
for but two houses
separated by several (p)lots.

neighbor(ing) dwellings,
bulldozed by eminency—
pissing contest between
would-be squatters
and government-lain burial cloth,

speak only fracture:
contract-haste
discoverable but by betrayed bits—
un-reclaimed sidewalks,
dead-end avenues.

town of should
wrapped in shroud;
sickly trees curl corpsed fingers,
hook wet wool sky down,
pull it snug.

something there was…
that now is not (but is);
visitors mistake travelers' abandoned
couches, mugs, jackets
for originals—

almost-altars:
once-offensive spectatorship
turned reminder—
daily eyesores to the stubborn two;
critical narrative inconsistency.

to plan a trip nowhere
or somewhere with nothing
is inaccurate (here);
absence, a palpable
please leave—

you have legs
that walk
eyes around their present,
what is presented,
what we, desecrator,
cannot see.

Ink has been writing creatively ever since the myriad avenues literature afford ripped his heart away from the rigid clutch of mathematics in high school. He's published in literary journals worldwide and, under his own power, produced four chapbooks as well as one complete collection: *Miserable with Fire*. Ink freelances as an editor for Piscataway House Publications, which published his work in a modern haiku/senryu collaboration as well as his 2014 collection, *Death Loves a Drinking Game*, as part of their Duel Book series.

www.ingramcontent.com/pod-product-compliance
Lightning Source LLC
LaVergne TN
LVHW021128080426
835510LV00021B/3357